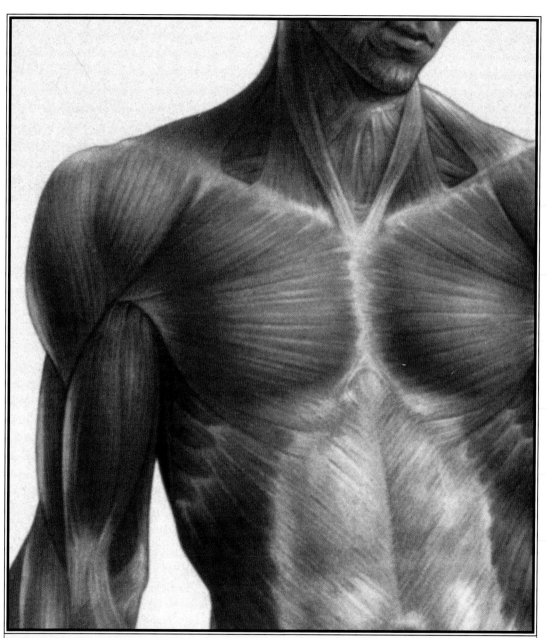

Muscles allow the human body to move around

THE *Muscles*

Anne Fitzpatrick

Smart Apple Media

◣ Published by Smart Apple Media

1980 Lookout Drive, North Mankato, MN 56003

Designed by Rita Marshall

Printed in the United States of America

◣ Pictures by Coreyography, LLC (Corey Rich), Getty Images/Time Life Pictures (Nat Farbman), Images International (Erwin C. "Bud" Neilson), Scott Leighton, Diane Meyer, Photo Researchers/Science Source (Biophoto Associates, John Daugherty, Parviz M. Pour), skjoldphotographs.com

◣ Library of Congress Cataloging-in-Publication Data

Fitzpatrick, Anne, 1978- The muscles / by Anne Fitzpatrick.

p. cm. — (The human body) Includes bibliographical references and index.

Summary: An introduction to different kinds of muscles and how they function.

◣ ISBN 1-58340-309-4

1. Muscles—Juvenile literature. [1. Muscles. 2. Muscular system.]

I. Title. II. Human body systems (Mankato, Minn.).

QM571 .F585 2003   611.73—dc21   2002030905

◣ First Edition 9 8 7 6 5 4 3 2 1

THE *Muscles*

Meet the Muscles   6

Kinds of Muscles   12

Muscle Motion   16

Muscle Health   19

Hands On: Make a Muscle   22

Additional Information   24

CONTENTS

Meet the Muscles

Muscles are for more than lifting weights. Muscles are used for walking and talking. They move food down a person's throat and grind it up in the stomach. They make eyes move back and forth and blink. Even while a person is sleeping, muscles are hard at work keeping the heart beating and the blood moving. Just about everything that goes on in a person's body uses a muscle. ➤ Muscles come in all sizes and shapes. Some are very small, such as the muscles of the

Lifting weights makes muscles bigger and stronger

eyes. The muscles in the legs must hold up the weight of the

whole body. They are large and powerful. Some of the muscles

in a person's back are shaped like small rings. They hold up the

spine, a row of bones along the center **The largest muscle is the gluteus maximus, in the buttock and thigh. The smallest is the stapedius, in the ear.** of the back. Muscles can be thin and flat, such as the muscles around the stomach. Others are long and narrow,

such as the muscles in the arms.

The muscles in a person's arms are long and narrow

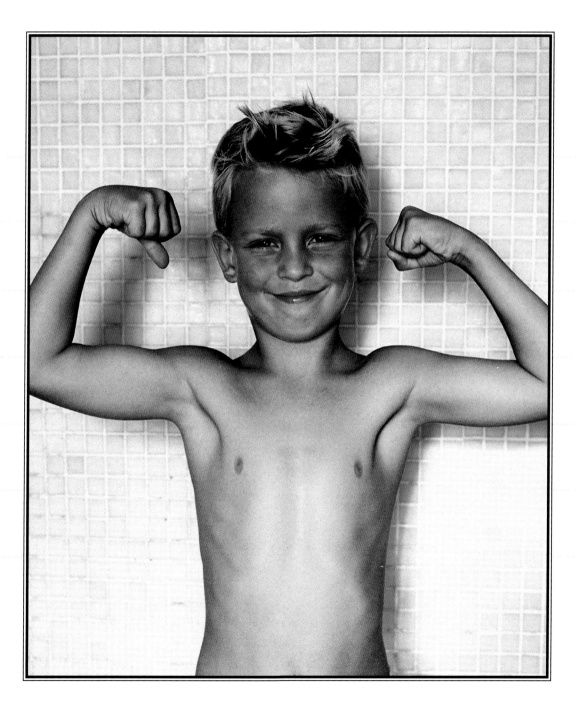

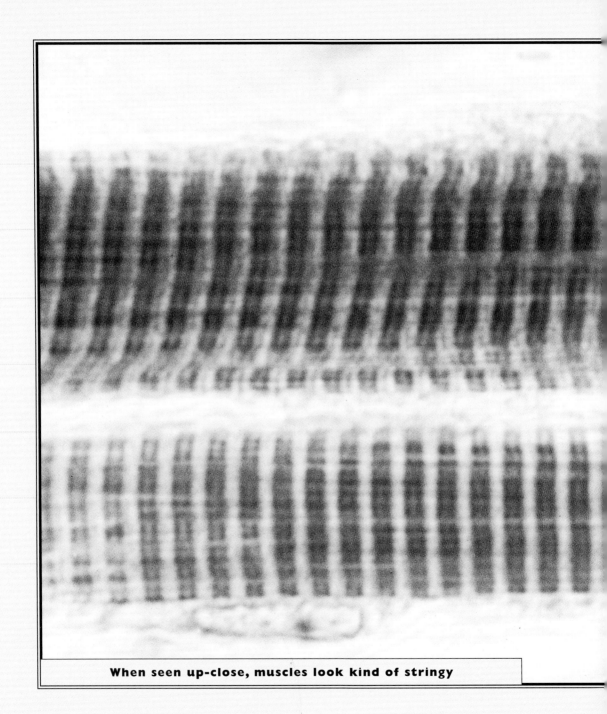

When seen up-close, muscles look kind of stringy

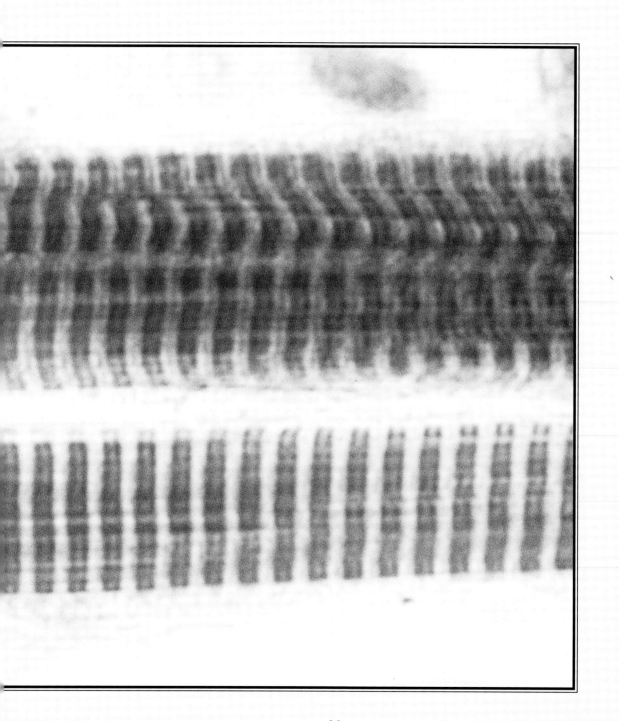

Kinds of Muscles

There are three kinds of muscles. **Skeletal muscles** make up about two-thirds of all the muscles in the body. They are called skeletal muscles because they are usually attached to the skeleton. Skeletal muscles are used for most movements, such as walking or lifting an arm. They look like tight bunches of tough strings.

There are more than 600 skeletal muscles in the human body, including about 30 found in just one hand.

Smooth muscles get their name because they are much smoother than skeletal muscles. They are found mainly in the

12

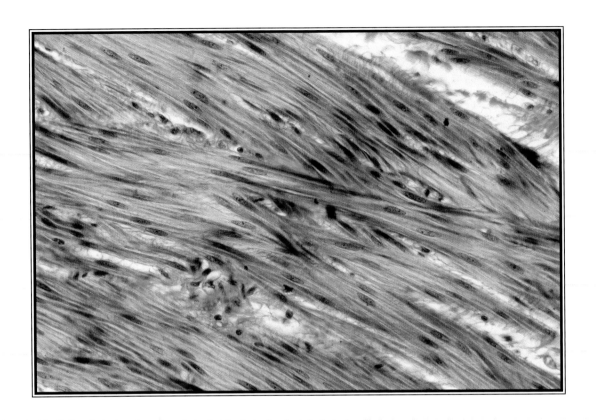

body's **organs**. A person cannot control the movements of

smooth muscles. They move blood and other fluids around the

body, grind up food in the stomach, and do all sorts of other

This is how smooth muscles look through a microscope

things that a person never thinks about. Smooth muscles can keep working hard longer than skeletal muscles, which usually get tired after a few minutes of hard work. ➤ **Cardiac muscles** never stop working hard. They are the muscles of the heart. Cardiac muscles **contract** about 60 to 90 times per minute. Each time they contract, the heart beats, and blood is pushed through the body. Cardiac muscles must keep the heart beating at all times to keep the blood moving. Cardiac muscles rest in between heartbeats, so they never get tired.

When the heart beats, it sends blood to other muscles

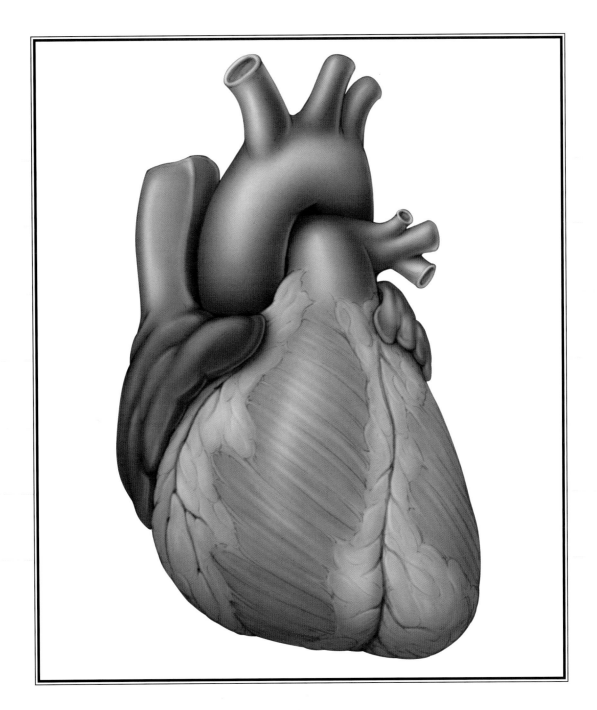

Muscle Motion

Muscles are used in many different ways. When the muscles of the face contract, people smile or frown. Muscles in the chest move the ribs in and out so that the lungs can fill with air. Some muscles stop things from moving. The muscles in the stomach area hold the organs in place. The muscles of the back hold the body up, so it is not pulled forward by the weight of the organs.

Muscles do not contract as easily after a person has been resting. Athletes often do warm-up exercises before a race or game.

Muscles let us smile, frown, and make funny faces

Many muscles work together in pairs. For example, there are two muscles in the arm called the biceps and the triceps. The biceps stretches from the shoulder to just below the elbow on the front of the arm. The triceps stretches along the back of the arm. When the biceps contracts, it pulls the lower part of the arm in. The arm bends. When the triceps contracts, it pulls the lower arm out. The arm straightens. Muscles in the hands, legs, and many other parts of the body also work in pairs.

The jaw muscle is one of the most powerful muscles in the body. It is strong enough to lift about 220 pounds (100 kg).

Muscle Health

Just as a car needs gas to run, the body needs food and

oxygen to keep the muscles going. Oxygen and bits of food are

In arm-wrestling, two people test their arm strength

carried to the muscles by the blood. That is why the heart beats faster when a person is working hard. The muscles need more food and oxygen. The heart pumps faster to get blood to the muscles that need it. ➤ Hard work is good for muscles. The more that muscles are used, the stronger they get. Exercise also makes sure that the muscles get lots of oxygen. Oxygen keeps muscles healthy and strong. Running, riding a bike, swimming, or rollerblading are some good ways to exercise the muscles. Keeping the muscles healthy is pretty fun!

Running and playing help muscles grow properly

Make a Muscle

This activity shows how the muscles in your arms work in pairs.

What You Need

A piece of cardboard   A pencil

Scissors   Two large rubber bands

What You Do

1. Draw a straight arm about 10 inches (25 cm) long on the cardboard. Cut it out and fold it in half.
2. Cut four small holes: two near the shoulder, and two just below the fold (elbow).
3. Cut the rubber bands. Make a knot (larger than the holes) at one end of each rubber band.
4. Thread a rubber band through one of the top holes and one of the bottom holes and knot it. Turn the arm over. Thread the second rubber band through the other two holes and knot it.

What You See

Pull on the rubber bands. They act like muscles, contracting to move your arm.

Healthy muscles make the body strong and flexible

Index

biceps 18

blood 6, 13, 14, 20

cardiac muscles 14

exercise 20

heart 6, 14, 20

oxygen 19–20

skeletal muscles 12

smooth muscles 12–14

triceps 18

Words to Know

cardiac muscles (KAR-dee-ak muh-sulz)—the muscles of the heart

contract (kun-TRAKT)—to pull in or become tighter

organs (OR-genz)—parts of the body with a particular job, such as the lungs, stomach, and eyes

skeletal muscles (SKEH-leh-tul muh-sulz)—muscles that work with bones; a person has control over their movement

smooth muscles (SMOOTH muh-sulz)—muscles a person cannot control; they are found mainly in organs

Read More

Angliss, Sarah. *Movers and Shapers: Muscles and Bones.* Thameside Press, 1999.

Llamas, Andreu. *Muscles and Bones.* Milwaukee: Gareth Stevens Publishing, 1998.

Simon, Seymour. *Muscles: Our Muscular System.* New York: Morrow Junior Books, 1998.

Internet Sites

BrainPOP Health: The Muscular System
http://www.brainpop.com/health/muscular/

Human Anatomy Online: The Muscular System
http://www.innerbody.com/image/musfov.html

Smartplay
http://www.smartplay.net/go_index.html